D1171434

FIGHTING FORCES ON LAND

M1126 STRYKER

DAVID BAKER

Rourke
Publishing LLC
Vero Beach, Florida 32964

© 2007 Rourke Publishing LLC

www.rourkepublishing.com

PHOTO CREDITS: All photos courtesy United States Department of Defense, United States Department of the Army

Title page: *Designated MCB-V, Stryker can carry a 120 mm mortar on a special carrier firing high explosive, infrared, infrared illumination, smoke, precision guided or conventional munitions.*

Editor: Robert Stengard-Olliges

Library of Congress Cataloging-in-Publication Data

Baker, David, 1944-
 M126 Stryker / David Baker.
   p. cm. -- (Fighting forces on land)
 Includes index.
 "Further Reading/Websites"
 ISBN 1-60044-246-3
 1. Stryker armored vehicle--Juvenile literature. I. Title. II. Series.
 UG446.5.B2348 2007
 623.7'475--dc22

                              2006010785

Printed in the USA

CG/CG

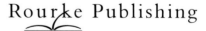

Rourke Publishing

www.rourkepublishing.com – sales@rourkepublishing.com
Post Office Box 3328, Vero Beach, FL 32964

TABLE OF CONTENTS

CHAPTER ONE

TRACKS OR WHEELS

When the US Army went in search of a light armored vehicle, or LAV, to replace the M113 Gavin armored **personnel** carrier it wanted wheels instead of tracks. There are advantages to having wheels rather than tracks.

▲

When the US Army went shopping for a replacement to the M113 Gavin Armored Personnel Carrier, it sought a more rugged, bigger and faster vehicle capable of carrying eight soldiers.

Although tracked vehicles have better off road **mobility** in sand, mud, and snow, wheeled vehicles have better speed and ride quality on primary and secondary roads. Moreover, they are usually quieter, faster, and can maneuver better and more responsively. To turn a corner, tracked vehicles need to stop one track while the other slews round. Operated by levers instead of a steering wheel, tracked vehicles have less **traction** on solid surfaces such as ice or metal.

▲
Unlike many other vehicles the Stryker has eight wheels. The front four wheels are linked together for steering, as seen here.

▲

This view of the rear shows the large hatchway and hinged door that doubles as a jump ramp. Continuous bench seating increases the adaptability of the interior, capable of carrying a stretcher if necessary.

Stryker crews have good vantage points to observe and return fire with light machine guns. The vehicle has protection against small caliber rounds and shrapnel but can be penetrated by rocket grenades and heavy machine guns at close range. ▶

The Gavin had a long history dating back to the 1960s when war involved massed armored divisions fighting off Soviet forces in northern Europe over open countryside in damp conditions. In the 21st century, the threat has changed and **urban** warfare in hot, dusty conditions is the new combat climate demanding very different vehicles.

7

CHAPTER TWO

A PEOPLE CARRIER

The heart of the requirement for a light armored vehicle is the Brigade Combat team (BCT). Brigade Combat teams fill the gap between heavy and light forces. The BCTs are highly mobile and self-sufficient. They need an armored vehicle to bring them and their equipment quickly into the battlefield.

▲

The driving position is relatively large for a vehicle of this size. Stryker is essentially a wedge-fronted box almost nine feet in width and height, a length of almost 23 ft and a loaded weight of 21 tons.

▲

The Stryker's design allows it to roll right off a plane or ship and into battle. Smoke mortars and machine gun mounting fold down for transit.

To carry out these duties the Army sought a vehicle bigger and more flexible than the old M113, which had performed well over four decades but was too old to keep pace with modern technologies.

Named in February 2002 after Stuart S. Stryker killed in World War II (1939-1945) and Robert F. Stryker killed in Vietnam during the 1960s, both of whom received the Medal of Honor, the M1126 is the latest and most flexible armored combat vehicle to enter service. It is one of the few vehicles to apply its name to units of the US Army, now known as Stryker Brigade Combat teams.

▲

The wedge shaped frontal area is designed to deflect incoming shells and the slatted armor is attached to pre-detonate shell heads and prevent the round contacting the steel surface of the vehicle.

▲

Sporting multiple smoke grenade mortars, the lead Stryker is loaded with equipment. The second vehicle carries a dual TOW anti-tank missile launcher top right.

CHAPTER THREE

Designed for Combat

Whereas the old M113 Gavin was built to carry people around the battlefield and support medium and heavy armored units, the Stryker is designed to be an **integral** part of combat. The Stryker is easily transported and is designed to drive straight off a C-130 military transport aircraft and into battle.

It comes in two versions, the Infantry Carrier Vehicle and the Mobile Gun System or MGS, although the latter is too big to fit inside a C-130.

▲

To a Stryker Brigade Team the vehicle itself can sometimes double as a shield against incoming fire. The small gun installed on the Stryker allows the vehicle to fit into a C-130 cargo plane.

▲

Although wheeled vehicles are considered more maneuverable, faster, and more agile than tracked vehicles, wheels are vulnerable to rocket propelled grenades and heavy machine guns.

Adaptability is the **cornerstone** of modern military weapon systems and vehicles have to be more adaptable than most. At its heart is the 350 hp diesel engine with six forward and one reverse gear driving eight road wheels with turning carried out through the four forward wheels.

▲

With snow chains on driving and steering wheels, a Stryker crew practices cold climate warfare, the wheeled vehicle is particularly good in these conditions.

On good surfaces, the vehicle can reach 60 mph and run for 300 miles on a single tank of fuel. The Stryker has a combat weight of 19 tons carrying a crew of two and a squad of six infantrymen. All Stryker versions share common parts and can adapt to various roles for different duties with a wide range of weapons and equipment.

▲

Aspects of the Stryker's layout and general configuration of hatches and access doors is similar to a wheeled version of the Bradley Infantry Fighting Vehicle, but with a top speed of more than 60 mph it is faster.

▲

The view from the top. A soldier holds a M240 7.62 mm machine gun at the ready covering the Stryker's rear.

Weighed in the Balance

The first production order for Stryker anticipated 2,100 vehicles to equip six BCTs. They were seen as urban street fighters where heavy armored brigades equipped with M1A1 Abrams main battle tanks or M2 Bradley fighting vehicles are difficult to employ effectively in narrow streets **flanked** by buildings.

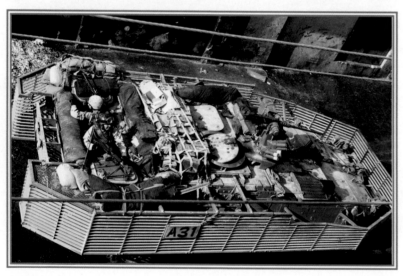

▲

This superb overhead shot displays the four optional gun positions on top of the Stryker's hull, with a 0.5 caliber machine gun and smoke grenade mortars toward the front.

▲

Like most armored vehicles in modern war, Strykers must be streetwise and capable of deploying soldiers quickly to local trouble spots and providing backup when they come under attack.

The first Stryker brigade arrived in Iraq during October 2003 and immediately ran into controversy over its lack of protection, vulnerability of exposed tires, and poor turning circle. Tracked vehicles can pivot whereas wheeled vehicles have to turn through a circle, a fact learned at cost in tight streets by those who thought that wheels were a better option.

▲

The Stryker is equipped with four of the new M6 quad-tube smoke mortars for lying down a screen of smoke to cover operations, hide soldiers, or as an evasion tactic.

In addition, the heavier weight applied to the ground compared to the flat weight distribution of a tracked vehicle was found to set off mines although tires survive the detonation better than track links.

▲

Stryker has good stability under load and has a low center of gravity that allows it to lean heavily, far beyond the tilt seen here as wheels hit a dirt-road depression.

▲

Because they are attached directly to the hatch, slatted steel armor blinds designed to pre-detonate incoming shells do not compromise rapid entry at the rear.

Despite surprises that **revealed** vulnerabilities in combat undetected by desk-top designers, Stryker brigades came to approve of their new mounts and modifications, including better protection from rocket propelled grenades and improved operational performance.

▲

A Stryker drives off a Boeing C-17 Globemaster III and, if necessary, goes straight into battle without the need for assembling weapons and guns, an essential tool in fast moving conflicts of the 21st century.

CHAPTER FIVE

MULTIPLE FUNCTIONS

Any modern weapons platform or military people carrier must earn its worth by doing several different jobs when those are needed and the Stryker is no exception.

▲

Strykers on mine clearance duty in Afghanistan.

In addition to being a medium armored vehicle and an infantry carrier, it can also be adapted for scout reconnaissance missions where squads of men are delivered to remote stations from where they move forward on foot to **reconnoiter** while the Stryker remains hidden in trees, brush, or some form of cover.

▲

Dual roles supporting infantry and serving as attack vehicles has compromised the concept and critics say the Stryker is unnecessary and that its jobs could be done by a combination of M113 and Bradleys.

▲

Sundown – and the work goes on.

Setting up or retrieving remotely operated sensors the squads can sneak in and out without detection.

The Stryker is also a command vehicle, medical evacuation vehicle, fire support, anti-tank, or engineer support vehicle. It is also possible to use the Stryker for sampling nuclear, biological, or chemical contamination carrying detectors that analyze the atmosphere and provide important warnings to the brigade.

▲
Crews take time out for a rest during an exercise.

CHAPTER SIX

Eyes for the Air Force

In August 2005, the US Air Force deployed its first Stryker unit to Iraq where it is used to cooperate with Army units on combined operations and to provide local weather **data** for pilots in strike and surveillance aircraft.

This information will also enable the Air Force to select the right aircraft to carry out essential support to ground units from the Army or the Marine Corps. In this way, Stryker is not only multifunctional but also valuable in operations carried out by US servicemen in different forces.

▲

A key aspect of the Stryker design requirment was that it could fit into the smallest US Air Force transport plane, the Lockheed Martin C-130 Hercules, and as this view shows that demand was met – just!

Glossary

cornerstone (KOR nur STONE) – a basic element or foundation

data (DAY tuh) – information or facts

flanked (FLANGKD) – to guard or to be at the side of something or someone

integral (IN tuh gruhl) – an essential part

mobility (MOH beel uh tee) – the ability to move

personnel (purss uh NEL) – a group of people who work for an organization

revealed (ri VEELD) – to make known, to show or bring into view

reconnoiter (ri CON noi ter) – to gather information about an enemy by physical observation

traction (TRAK shuhn) – the friction or gripping power that keeps a vehicle from slipping

urban (UR buhn) – having to do with a city

INDEX

FURTHER READING

Vick, A., Orletsky, D., Pirnie, B., and Jones, Seth. *The Stryker Brigade Combat Team*. Rand Corporation, 2002

Zaloga, Stephen. *BMP: Infantry Combat Vehicle*. Motorbooks, 1990

WEBSITES TO VISIT

http://www.globalsecurity.org/military/systems/ground/mav.htm
http://www.army-technology.com/projects/stryker

ABOUT THE AUTHOR

David Baker is a specialist in defense and space programs, author of more than 60 books and consultant to many government and industry organizations. David is also a lecturer and policy analyst and regularly visits many countries around the world in the pursuit of his work.